LITERATURE OF
THE GRAVEYARD

JEAN-PAUL SARTRE

FRANÇOIS MAURIAC

ANDRÉ MALRAUX

ARTHUR KOESTLER

by Roger Garaudy

MEMBER OF THE FRENCH NATIONAL
ASSEMBLY

INTERNATIONAL PUBLISHERS, NEW YORK

PN
773
G32

CONTENTS

Translated from the French
by Joseph M. Bernstein

INTRODUCTION

"We have given you, Adam . . ."

For four centuries now, morality as well as political power has, for many men, ceased to exist "by divine right." If man no longer has as a guide to his action the will of God, revealed in a Book and interpreted by an infallible Church, he must himself look for the rules of his conduct, with his own ends and means.

As early as the Renaissance, Pico della Mirandola posed this problem in his *Treatise on the Greatness of Man*. And he imagined nature addressing man in the following words:

"We have given you, Adam, neither a definite dwelling nor a specific face nor a special function, so that you may choose the dwelling, face, and function that you wish. We have placed you in the center of the world, in order that you may more easily look all around you in the world; we have made of you neither a celestial being nor an earthbound being, neither an immortal nor a mortal, so that you yourself may mold and shape like a sculptor the form you prefer to give yourself. You can plunge into the lower ranks of brutes or lift yourself into the higher ranks of divine beings."

As for us, we realize more and more clearly that, in the words of Marx, "men make their own history." Hence every philosophy that is not subordinated to religion begins necessarily with a meditation on freedom. The French Revolution of 1789 was the first attempt at a practical solution of this problem.

With the Revolution, this philosophy of freedom, by taking hold of the masses of the people, became a fighting and effective philosophy. And since then, this problem of freedom has become the center of all our political and philosophical debates. That is the guiding thread I have chosen for my criticism; for it is this problem which delimits present-day philosophical positions.

FALSE PROPHET: JEAN-PAUL SARTRE

Sartre poses the problem exactly as I have just posed it, and as it is posed to all those for whom God is no more. He recalls the phrase uttered by Kirilov in Dostoyevsky's *The Possessed*: "If God did not exist, everything would be allowed." And Sartre adds: "That is the point of departure of existentialism." Thus, Sartre's meditation on freedom begins with the nihilist postulate. Either God surrounds me and commands me, or I am in the void. Either man is in God or man is in the void. Sartre chooses man in the void.

"Our point of departure is the subjectivity of the history of the individual," he asserts, invoking the name of Descartes. And he erects a philosophy of the *tabula rasa*.*

"Men make their own history," said Marx, but he added: "but they do not make it just as they please; they do not make it under circumstances chosen by themselves, but under circumstances directly found, given and transmitted from the past."†

That is where our disagreement with existentialism begins.

Thought, when it is cut off from action, is sick. This sickness is sometimes called mythology, mysticism, idealism. Today it is called existentialism.

For it is indeed a sickness. Roquentin explains his "nausea" to us in the novel of the same name: "Objects begin to exist in your hand." We doubt whether a machinist thus suddenly discovers the existence of his tools. Roquentin's point of view

* Literally, "clean slate," referring to the mind before receiving impressions.—*Ed.*

† Karl Marx, *The Eighteenth Brumaire of Louis Bonaparte*, p. 13, New York.—*Ed.*

is that of the sick persons described by Dr. Pierre Janet. The latter shows how they have lost "the function of the real": basing themselves on their "maladjustment," they build a metaphysics. Their central problem is constantly posed in the following terms: Why does something rather than nothing exist? Do I really exist? And do the things that surround me exist? Those are the fundamental themes of existentialism; and Sartre's thesis on *Being and Nothingness** remains within this realm of metaphysical pathology. The healthy man's philosophy begins beyond that point.

The world in disorder of the bourgeoisie cannot, at the risk of death, allow intelligence to have the upper hand. In order to perpetuate chaos, prudence dictates that thinking be exiled into a world of abstraction. When every intellectual begins to revolve in his shining metaphysical bubble like a squirrel in its cage, the social system no longer runs any risk. And everyone is satisfied: our philosopher rejoices at his "freedom" and the social system at its "security."

The Resistance movement forced many of the sleep-walking intellectuals to awaken. Sartre was one of them. He finally had the feeling that he was going to be able to make something of his freedom. "Never were we freer than under the German occupation," he wrote nostalgically in the publication, *Les Lettres Françaises,* in September 1944. Then, he explains, it was a question of "saying no." And even that is symptomatic: to be free means to refuse. That is the point of view of those who belong to the past: freedom is negation. For those who march toward the future, freedom means adherence and building. Sartre, and those who resemble him, found in the Resistance movement a greater isolation: "This total responsibility, in total solitude, is it not the very unfolding of our freedom?" he asked in the same article.

And when there was no longer anything to deny, or rather when the most important thing was to stop denying, what was one to do with one's freedom? That freedom, which was

* English titles are given wherever they exist in translation.—*Ed.*

8

nothing but isolation and refusal, turned out to be a formless freedom. Sartre and his kind never felt themselves part of the masses, one with men and their history. So to him freedom is not creative participation in the dialectics of necessity. To rejoin the ranks, one must make an arbitrary leap—as irrational as the "fall" of Epicurus's atoms—outside the metaphysical cage. "A man does not exist in the manner of a tree or a pebble"; he must "make himself a worker," Sartre asserted in his initial article in *Temps Modernes.*

Commenting on the definition of existentialism ("for man, existence precedes essence"), Sartre writes: "Man rises up in the world and defines himself afterward." We willingly grant him that man has no "definition" in the logical sense of the term, that is, he does not possess an aggregate or *eternal* system of attributes and characteristics. But he has a past—and a clearly determined past. Man, in the words of the poet Ponge, is *not only the future of man;* he is *also* the past of man.

To omit that is to doom us to immobility and impotence, for it means that we have cut off the two living roots of our freedom: history and knowledge. *Uprooted from history, freedom is nothing but an ineffective ersatz.*

We are not naked savages without a past, arriving in a virgin forest in order to "choose" to be free. History exists, and we are at the end of its sharply defined trajectory. It is our springboard from which to go forward toward a higher freedom.

We are neither the only ones nor the first ones to travel "the roads of freedom." Some have begun to clear the ground, others are clearing it around us. We are heirs of history. And history means other people, the dead and the living; they have handed down to us equipment and techniques which are imperfect but which do exist. They are called the social system; and they co-ordinate the efforts of man, even though they are doing it rather badly at the moment.

In a word, freedom is not a gift from heaven placed in my cradle, but a job begun by others, and at which I will work more effectively the more intelligently I associate myself with others in the collective workshop of history. By omitting history, existentialism dooms us to the stone-headed ax of primitive man or to the solitude of the artisan in clearing the roads of freedom. Several thousand years of human history have taught us more effective methods.

But, some will say, I am free to join your collective workshop or not to join it, and therein lies my total responsibility, my absolute choice. Sartre writes that any given worker "is free since he can always choose to accept his lot with resignation or revolt against it."

But if this choice is as completely free and timeless as he would have us believe, how explain the fact that as the contradictions in capitalist society sharpen, the overwhelming majority of workers chooses a revolutionary position? And is it not exceptional for a big capitalist to rally to the revolution?

It can only be explained by the fact that the individual's role in production, that is, the class to which he belongs, determines in a very great measure his choice. So the decision is no longer absolute and timeless; it flows from the realization of certain necessities. Between myself and freedom, there is knowledge.

At this point the second condition for freedom intervenes: science. *Freedom is borne by science like a plant on its stalk.* An irrational freedom rising in the chaos of a world without laws dooms us to impotence, that is, to slavery and despair.

This formless freedom makes for a history that is unforeseeable and without structure. One cannot judge an individual before the series of his acts is ended, in other words, before his death. That is the central theme of Sartre's play, *No Exit.* And since we have not yet had the honor to see the human race die, we cannot judge its history. "The sense of the social past is perpetually in reprieve." (*Being and Nothingness.*) This is a serious matter, for if our past is so spineless and shapeless, if everything changes its meaning at every moment, we are left disarmed in the face of the future. If there is no scientific knowledge of history, there can be no effective techniques in politics.

Thus we see the chief failing of existentialism: indifference to science. To Sartre it is a hereditary failing: the heritage of Kierkegaard and Nietzsche weighs heavily on these epigones of existentialism. Willy-nilly, their apology for "subjectivity" develops quickly into a contempt for science. In Sartre, freedom, which is an absolute choice, has nothing to do with reason; history, drowned in subjectivity and the perpetual waiting for a justification that never comes, has nothing to do with science. This should suffice to expose the basically obscurantist character of existentialism. And this obscurantism, despite Sartre's atheism, will lead more young people to religious faith than to militant action.

Already I can hear some objecting: "Your materialism makes of man an object, a thing; it destroys his freedom and his individual dignity." For a hundred and fifty years the Catholic Church has repeated this argument against all revolutionary materialists. And is it not a paradox and an arrant denial of historical experience to make such a reproach against the materialist philosophy? Have not two centuries of persecution, from the Encyclopedists to Gracchus Babeuf and from Blanqui to the Marxists, aroused the greatest heroism and sacrifices in the battles for freedom?

To oppose materialism and freedom, determinism and freedom, means to make a caricature of materialism and determinism. In *Temps Modernes,* Sartre defines matter as follows: "What characterizes matter is its inertia. That means that it is incapable of producing anything by itself. A vehicle of movements and energy, these movements and this energy always come to it from the outside: it borrows them and yields them."

In an article written some time ago, the late Paul Langevin commented that such a definition lagged two thousand years behind the development of the sciences. Lucretius (following Epicurus) concretized this image: an infinity of tiny pebbles falling in the void and deviating from each other according to the elementary laws of friction. To insert freedom into this mechanism, Lucretius needed a miracle, a break with this mechanism which, in his eyes, defined reason. He called this

11

miracle, this irrational element, the *clinamen* (the inclination of a thing). It is the same irrational and the same miracle that Sartre seeks when he asks for "this little bit of withdrawal which is indispensable to man in order to dominate the determinism of his life."

But Sartre no longer has the same excuse as Lucretius. For two thousand years of scientific progress have given us a less simplified picture of determinism and matter. In order to live and make progress in the production of his means of existence, man needs "a science which will make him master and possessor of nature." He must know the laws of nature in order to know at what point in the chain he has to insert his personal action so as to mold nature according to his needs.

This knowledge of the connections between the phenomena of nature is called determinism. And the cause is that link upon which I can act: it therefore varies according to the complexity of the image of the world I possess and according to my means of intervention, that is to say, according to the degree of progress in science and technology. So this knowledge of the connections between the phenomena of nature does not have an immutable definition: it is modified and refined with every great scientific discovery.

At the time of Descartes, following his discoveries in analytic geometry, the algebraic function furnished the model for this knowledge; and in that period, in which Vaucanson's *automata* were the last word in technology, many felt that all things were connected in nature as the various parts of a machine are connected with one another.

Such a definition did not exhaust and, above all, did not arrest the notion of determinism. Mechanistic determinism was only a stage, a moment in the conception of nature and its laws. Scientific methods, dealing with increasingly complex objects, have enriched the concept of determinism and made it more flexible. As Langevin noted, it is not a question of a retreat from or a disavowal of determinism; for now one perceives more connections and handles them with more sureness and power.

Biology, then sociology and history, have allowed us to form a richer idea of determinism, which includes in the domain over which it rules both the perpetual creation of life and the statistical determinism of social phenomena such as suicide, unemployment, crime, and prostitution. And all the other sciences have benefited from these new researches. Physics in its turn is using statistical determinism; and the current conception of matter makes of it a permanent center of creation and destruction similar to life.

Since, in the age of the atom-bomb, we have a different idea of matter and determinism from that obtaining in the period of Vaucanson's *automata*, science permits us to substitute a chain of more complex notions for the metaphysical polar notions of mechanistic determinism and absolute free will. These notions, moreover, are more in line with everyday experience and with that of the sciences. Between these two limits, man is neither a robot nor a miracle-maker. His freedom is not opposed to determinism—only the latter nourishes it.

Of course, in the development of our science as of our history there are moments, if not of rupture, at least of uncertainty. Or rather, moments of less certain and less probable choice. They are not the stuff of my moral life. They do not even have a place of outstanding dignity in moral life; they are the slag. They reveal temporary gaps, either in my personal intelligence or in science.

I am freer the more lucid and the better informed I am; I am freer when I can say with more certainty: I cannot choose otherwise. Spinoza, and after him Hegel, taught us that to be free means to bear within ourselves all the reasons for our action.

To be sure, reason is not to us what it was to them: that is, an eternal reality, independent of the efforts of science and technology to mold it each day. The necessity that determines our action is often only approximate, as is our knowledge itself. But what remains true is that the more perfect this approximation is, the more compulsive our knowledge becomes. And on the day when there is finally no opaqueness either in our social relations or in our relations with nature, on that day the dream of Socrates will come true. This necessity, all the more compulsive in that it is more "reasonable," is the highest form of freedom. It is what Engels called "the leap from the kingdom of necessity into the kingdom of freedom."

So to us Marxists, freedom means a greater power over nature, over social relations, and over ourselves. In this respect, it is the measure of progress in knowledge and society. It is essentially affirmation and creation; it means building for the future. That is why socially this concept of freedom is the attribute of builders and not grave-diggers (as history confirms). It is the philosophy of those who love the future, who call it forth and prepare it, knowing in advance that it belongs to them. This was true of men like Helvetius and Diderot, materialist philosophers who were spokesmen of the bourgeoisie on the eve of the Great French Revolution. It is true today of the working class, convinced in its turn that the future belongs to it, since 1848 with Marx and Engels, since 1917 with Lenin and Stalin.

Having turned his back on science, Sartre can no longer return to action. He can neither furnish nor even accept an effective method of transforming reality. In truth, having abandoned *en route* everything that can make freedom rational and our history scientific, Sartre allows the minds of his disciples to wander between a subjectivity without laws and a world without structure. Then what becomes of objectivity in this universe without rules? It simply fades out. Sartre rejects materialism and yet claims that he avoids idealism. Here we see the futility of that impossible "third party." Phenomenalism is an unstable position, but in Sartre it is not ambiguous: it sinks completely into idealism, and into the worst of idealisms, which does not preserve that solid rational framework which Hegel succeeded in giving to it.

This very sketchy outline of existentialism, in which we have merely indicated several of its characteristic points, allows us to define this philosophy with respect to Marxism.

14

Sartre wrote some time ago in *Action* that he was not far "from the conception of man to be found in Marx." His ambition was "to complete Marxism on the side of subjectivity."

But existentialism does not complete Marxism, it contradicts Marxism. From its doctrine of free will to its idealist theory of knowledge, from its negation of scientific history to its indifference toward science, existentialism castrates man. It deprives him of his liberating weapons: the science of the world and the science of man. And the revolution is only a word if it is not first of all science. The free man or revolutionary is not he who discovers within himself, as a possibility of personal adventure, the power to deny or to "reduce to nothingness," as Sartre would say, but he who, having made of science "his very flesh" (to use an expression of Lenin), measures his freedom by the power of social construction in which he participates.

By this mirage of a solitary and formless freedom, attractive to human beings without roots and impotent with despair, Sartre leads our students into a dead-end. His play, *The Flies,* expresses pathetically the anguish of too many bloodless intellectuals who look for something real beyond their culture: "I live in the air . . . I am all alone," Orestes cries, and he begs for the "joy of going somewhere." Sartre cannot go beyond this abstract aspiration to the concrete.

His spineless world has lost its object. His freedom has lost its content. And he leaves naked and starving those he has found mutilating their old clothes and vomiting forth their old food. Nothing in his philosophy opens the road to action. That is why this philosophy is profoundly reactionary. It shunts those it affects onto a kind of siding.

As a matter of fact, the "ravages" of existentialism are very limited: it is not an epidemic that can grip a whole nation. This thinking severed from the real world has no hold on the working class, which is today the bearer of the golden rule of philosophy: thought is born of action, is action, serves action. It involves at most a titillation or mild fever affecting a few intellectuals who considered themselves "demobilized" after the Resistance movement had played its part. Cut off from the broad masses of the people, they like to make a god of their confusion and their "nothingness"; and, believing that they cannot find a goal worthy of their talents, they are satisfied with ersatzes and bargain-counter revolutions. It is up to Marxism to teach our intellectuals that they have something better to do than to project into the absolute their own contradictions, which are those of capitalist society, and something better than to allow their desire for a full life to evaporate in metaphysical smoke.

What about the others, you may ask? What about the classes that are in decline and no longer have the future on their side? To their spokesmen, freedom always appears as an irrational break with determinism. Freedom is refusal and negation. But what can it promise and construct for someone who has no future? This ersatz freedom, without content and without laws, is nothing but an impotent revolt and an evasion of sordid and desperate reality.

The most striking and also the *finest* literary expression of this view of the world is that offered to us in the works of François Mauriac.

GREAT WRITER IN BONDAGE:
FRANÇOIS MAURIAC

I would like to be fair to François Mauriac, for he taught me revolt. Not revolution, just revolt—for he was able, at times, to say: "No!" But I have had to look beyond him and against him for affirmation, for adherence to a cause and joy in adherence.

No matter! His refusals had greatness and I must really thank him for them, for he won them with difficulty. His first experience was that of acceptance and dependence. "As for myself," he writes in *God and Mammon*: "I belong to the race of those who, born in Catholicism, realized as soon as they reached adulthood that they could never escape it, that it was not given them to leave it or return to it. They were in it, they remain in it, they will remain in it forever. . . . I was born a Catholic; I did not choose. That religion was imposed on me from birth."

One is reminded of Maurice Barrès in his *Scenes and Doctrines of Nationalism*. Yet Barrès spoke of another God: "I have never had any other ideas save those in which I have been immersed since birth. . . . There is not even freedom to think. I can only live according to my dead. . . . I have been horrified at my dependence, at my inability to create."

Alluding to Barrès in a study of Mauriac, I do not know if I begin at the beginning or at the end; for Barrès was his first teacher and it was to him that Mauriac, in 1945, dedicated his book: *La Rencontre avec Barrès* (*The Meeting with Barrès*). "To the young people of my generation," he writes, "Barrès offered a theory." And discussing his life as a student, Mauriac reveals in a few words all the secrets of his intellectual development: "Thanks to a modest income, I was financially

17

independent. . . . Barrès was my best teacher. My religious education had disposed me to listen to his teachings."

Mauriac's great merit is that he has been more sincerely a man of Gironde than Barrès was a man of Lorraine. No one has described with more power the landed gentry of the Landes region or the merchants of Bordeaux. He is not, like Balzac, the chronicler of French society in its entirety, but only of a clan. *Préséances* (*Precedences*) depicted the rich merchants only from the outside, from the point of view of vanity; *Vipers' Tangle* reveals them from within, from the point of view of greed. He lays bare the motives of a class in which, according to Balzac, "the hundred-sou piece is embedded in every conscience and clinks in every sentence." With *Vipers' Tangle*, Mauriac reaches his high point. He tears away all masks: those of the bourgeois family, those of property, and those of the "right-minded." Not since Balzac's *Cousin Pons* have the jealousies, covetousness, and hatreds of a "family drama" revolving around a fortune been illuminated with so sharp a light. The novelist must have had a discerning hatred of his environment to teach us to hate it so strongly.

The first limitation of Mauriac is this narrowness in his field of human experience. Unlike Balzac, he is incapable of embracing a world. As soon as one of his characters leaves the Gironde region, and especially the upper bourgeoisie of the Gironde, he becomes nothing but a pale and shadowy phantom. As Mauriac himself acknowledges: "No drama can begin to live in my mind if I do not locate it in the places where I have always lived." And the results of this limitation, as we shall see, go beyond the artistic.

Moreover, Mauriac has built his system on this basis. In his *Romancier et Ses Personnages* (*The Novelist and His Characters*), he asserts: "Why condemn oneself to describe an environment one does not know well? The truth of the matter is that it is not very important whether one introduces a duchess, a woman of the bourgeoisie, or a charwoman: the essential point is to achieve human truth. . . . The truth that we must achieve is like a subterranean stream which rises to the surface of the life of a society woman as well as that of a woman beset by poverty. Every one of us digs at the spot where he is, where he has lived."

Mauriac is the painter of this bourgeoisie of the Gironde. He paints it with passion, with the passion of hate, without ever relinquishing this bourgeoisie, this passion and hate.

Furthermore, he is convinced that there exists an "eternal" man, and that it is enough to scratch the top surface of a social class or a historic period to find an immutable core of humanity: "Beyond the distortions which our poor daily tasks impose on all of us, the wise and the ignorant, on workers and writers, on society ladies and workingwomen and women of every stripe, this being vibrates, *always the same in every epoch*. It suffers, renounces, is jealous, murders, or sacrifices itself."

This classic myth of the eternal man confirms him in his unconscious dependence on his own clan: his view of the world, so narrowly conditioned by his education in Catholic schools and by his bourgeois environment in the Gironde, seems to him an "eternal" necessity. "As soon as I sit down to work, everything is colored according to my eternal colors."

Such as it is, his description of the big merchants of Bordeaux and the landed proprietors of the Landes region is great and powerful. As Balzac said: "It is not the author's fault if things speak by themselves and speak so loudly."

Mauriac's misfortune is that he has never moved out of his class. When he judges it and detests it, he is still looking "from the inside." And the bourgeoisie does not go beyond this "inside." It gives birth to its own grave-diggers but does not carry them within itself. From the inside, the most one can feel is "disgust"; and there lies the tragedy of Mauriac.

He exists in a world which he can only despise. And he remains chained to that world. His two greatest characters belong body and soul to that world. Thérèse Desqueyroux in *Thérèse* has property in her blood: she marries Bernard for his two thousand hectares of pine forest in the Landes country; and the hero of *Vipers' Tangle* is a spiritual son of Balzac's Grandet and a grandson of Molière's Harpagon.

But Mauriac has put the best of himself in these two heroes: they too are immersed in a world which they hate. They are Mauriac's allegory. By poisoning Bernard, Thérèse would like to murder "her milieu, her climate"—the one to which Mauriac belongs and which he would like to destroy. The old man in *Vipers' Tangle* finally tears himself away from his greed only in the illuminating final ten pages of the novel. He dies a little too soon to recite the Lord's Prayer or to redeem his life with a sign of the Cross and a drop of holy water like Daniel Trassis, the Don Juan in *Fleuve de Feu* (*River of Fire*).

Mauriac gives us the key to his two favorite characters: "The hero of *Vipers' Tangle* and the murderess, Thérèse Desqueyroux, as horrible as they may appear, are without the one thing in the world which I hate and which I find it hard to endure in a human being: complacency and smugness. They are not satisfied with themselves; they know their own wretchedness." (*The Novelist and His Characters*.)

His men and women avid for profit always end by making some slight gesture of denial with their stubborn faces. Then Mauriac's novel stops: he has found one of God's creatures beneath the Pharisee girded with selfishness and wealth. This individual is no longer a criminal, but a sinner. He is aware of his abjectness. He is a human "person."

Mauriac's theology does not go much further than that. "At the age when the blood awakens," he confesses in *God and Mammon*, "everything crystallizes around notions of purity, sin, and the state of grace." Since then the creative artist has grown; his vision, sharpened by rancor and hate, has penetrated further and more deeply. But his metaphysics remains that of a choir boy.

In truth, this reproach will scarcely affect him. For in that field he has no pretensions as a philosopher; he is an artist. "Thanks to a certain gift for atmosphere," he tells us in his *Journal*, "I try to make the Catholic universe of evil perceptible, palpable, and tangible. This sinner, of whom the theologians give us an abstract idea, is embodied in myself."

In all this, I am not attempting to detract from Mauriac's

worth. By the impact of the characters he has created, he has flung a challenge at his models: he has had the will power not to leave them intact. I do not know if any of "his kind" have taken his accusations to heart. But he denounced the Pharisees of his race simply by drawing their portrait. He was able to say "No!" to their most characteristic acts; he said "No!" to the bloody butchers of Badajoz and the murderers of Guernica. He protested more against the sacrilege than the inhumanity. What of it? By protesting against the insult to God, he protested against the violence unleashed against the Spanish people—and that was one way to be on the side of man.

Yes, he was able to say: "No!" But the tragedy of Mauriac, the tragedy of the men of his class, is that they cannot go beyond this negation. He denounces the inhumanity of the social system, but he does not see any force on which to rely in order to go beyond this inhuman system. He glimpsed this for a moment during the Resistance. Then he wrote: "Only the working class, in the main, remained faithful to desecrated France." But it was not enough to understand: he had to choose. He would have had to say "yes" to too many things he did not know, to too many men he feared.

He was not able to do so. So the editorial writer of *Figaro*, tortured in the face of an inhuman world he cannot accept, and cut off from the only force capable of leading to victory the battle against this disorder, has withdrawn into his shell, a stifling and ignoble shell, but "his shell."

Chained to this world he has never ceased to despise and which he passionately defends, Mauriac is doomed to despair. It is true that if the world were limited to that bourgeois clan by which Mauriac's social experience is delimited, we ought really to despair of man and his future. Knowing only the bourgeois philistinism of man and believing that he sees in it the eternal man with his no less eternal "sin," he has developed the most frightful contempt for the people. Hence his respect for the most outmoded conceptions of the élite and the leader, his aversion to democracy, his fear of the masses, his sneers at "the man of the masses," his sneers at "the new man," his hatred for political parties or countries in which men have fundamentally changed. This new and mocking Ecclesiast, with his despair and contempt for man, gives us an amazing example of the dependence of a writer on his environment. That is what a class and a social order have been able to do with our artists. In their freedom as writers, they depict more powerfully than any other a sordid world to which they completely belong. They have been able to communicate to us their passion and their indignation, and to teach us to say no, once and for all. And Mauriac, unable to discern the new man who is coming to birth, remains captive of the world he has never been able to leave. When a new world rose up before him, he drew back, he withdrew into the shelter he had so often cursed, and fearfully took refuge there. Today he has nothing but the poor reflexes of his class. He bears within himself its corpse, which no longer fills him with horror.

The novelist has never been able to kill Thérèse Desqueyroux, but politics has let her die or forgotten her. Her revolt is quite dead. Every day the fearless author of *Vipers' Tangle* fades a little more behind the outraged and trembling editorial writer of *Figaro*.

In *God and Mammon,* laying proud claim to his responsibility as a writer, he defined his profession: "Thus I continued to work within Catholicism, an object of suspicion, if not of contempt and disapproval, for my brothers." Now everything has returned to normal: Mauriac has again found "his" kind. He is no longer a target of their scandal or anger. He shares their opinion on communism, democracy, and the Soviet Union. The philanthropic old ladies are willing to shut their eyes on his past. They are charitable enough to forgive "all." At last he has become "*the* Catholic writer," occupying the position that Henri Bordeaux once held.

Every morning the Maucoudinat and Desqueyroux families wax ecstatic as they read his article in *Figaro;* they thank God for having made the prodigal son return to the fold. Mauriac has only had to slip down the inclined plane; at the very bottom he has rejoined his class.

The example of Mauriac is not an isolated one, and conveys an important lesson. Negation and refusal are not revolutionary. Experience has taught us that it is not enough to call oneself anti-capitalist if one really means to work to get rid of capitalism. Anyone may term himself anti-capitalist, but this "refusal" does not commit him to anything.

If Marx's *Capital* has genuinely revolutionary value, it is not because it denounces the evils of the capitalist system. Others denounced these evils before him, without affecting the system in the slightest. If Marx has genuinely revolutionary value, it is because in his materialist analysis of the relation of forces, he revealed not only the inner contradictions of the capitalist system but also the force capable of overcoming these contradictions and creating a new social system—the working class. That is the only force capable of leading to its final conclusion the struggle for the destruction of this inhuman system.

Marx's dialectical materialism does not permit any evasions: it is a question of settling a historic conflict. Man wrests his freedom from the chaos of capitalism; in this jungle of appetites and dog-eat-dog competition in which freedom is but a dream and a juggling of phrases, he can only win his freedom through class struggle.

And we must not "play around" with the word "commitment." To commit oneself, without dodging or evading, means only one thing concretely: to take part in the struggle of the progressive forces, the vanguard of which is the working class.

"Happy are those," wrote Maxim Gorky, "who know that the people are an inexhaustible source of energy and are able to transform all the possible into the necessary, all dreams into reality. For they never stop feeling their flesh-and-blood link with the people; and to them, it is a source of life and creation. This feeling grows within them and fills their heart with great joy and with the need to create new forms of culture."

All the cleverness of the grave diggers consists in finding, for young people seeking a way out, a solution which is not revolutionary. In this respect, the case of André Malraux is especially significant.

THE DEATH MASK OF ANDRÉ MALRAUX

André Malraux is the central character and indeed the sole character of his books. In his novels it is his own face he contemplates as if in a multiple mirror. Everything else—other human beings, nations, classes with their torments and hopes, their defeats or their revolutions—only serves as a background to set in relief a profile designed to be triumphant or tragic.

He is capable of describing a landscape—then nonchalantly, he adds this detail: "Further off, the armies of Central Asia advance like a whirlwind." (*Tentation de l'Occident—Temptation of the West*, p. 16.) Or he offers definitions like these: "Dynamite it was—the good old romantic weapon of the Asturianos!" (*Man's Hope*, p. 13); "Spain was that twisted machine-gun on an Arab's coffin and his birds numbed with cold crying in the ravines." (*Ibid.*, p. 482.) These are the "ingredients" of every one of Malraux's novels: himself and a "background" designed to reveal him. A novel by Malraux is an extended reportage interlarded with philosophical dialogues between the author and variants of himself.

Here I am not criticizing the writer's talent, which is undeniably great, but the man who expresses himself in his art. This man interests me because he bears witness to an era, to a class, and to its decadence of which he is the fine flower. If he is a powerful artist, it is because he has admirably matched his backgrounds with his personality. Malraux offers us the complete prism of himself against an apocalyptic background.

THE NERO COMPLEX

Like an idol, a Buddha gazing at his navel, he demands human sacrifices: Malraux only sees himself sniffing the odor of blood. Hence, this existentialist philosopher became a war correspondent. *The Conquerors, Man's Hope, Wrestling with the Angel*—they all present a blood-and-thunder film with cries, battles, victories, and, above all, defeats; and with crowds of fighters (who in Malraux are crowds of extras without problems). In the quiet interludes of this gory film, we come upon intellectuals beset with problems who need this climate, this excitement, in order to meditate about themselves. In the midst of the battle Malraux sits about in a circle with himself, his variants, and his potential selves. His nostrils dilated by the slaughter, he falls into a trance and draws from the clay of these nameless and tortured masses the spark of the Spirit. As on the Greek temples or in Homer, above the epic frescoes the assembled gods sit. But the god's problems are quite far removed from those of the men in whose battles he has participated for one moment, in order to sense their intoxication. His problems are very different from the problems of those who fight (and who, first of all, do not despair as he does, otherwise they would not fight). Moreover, the people who hearken to the god's oracles are not to be found among the fighters whom he has chosen as his characters, but rather among those who do not fight or who fight against the fighters.

It is no accident, as we shall see, that the Catholic newspaper, *La Croix*, greets this "tragic atheist" with deep sympathy; that now, at the beginning of 1948, Malraux has replaced Jean-Paul Sartre in circles that are looking for a revolutionary ideology which does not lead to revolution; and that, in short, this "Red" is the favorite son of the reactionaries. The world of the bored and especially the world of the frightened—the world of decadence—needs an ersatz type of spiritual adventure for the titillation of its inner life; and even more than that, it needs "spiritual revolutions" in order to avoid real ones and to sidetrack demands for social change.

A decadent class that still persists in calling itself the "élite" has found in Malraux its most brilliant "medium." In a lecture given November 4, 1946, at the Sorbonne, Malraux posed this problem: "On this soil of Europe, yes or no, is man dead?" And he added this comment: "At the end of the nineteenth century the voice of Nietzsche again uttered the ancient cry heard on the Archipelago: God is Dead! . . . and he restored to that phrase all its tragic meaning. What that meant was very well known: it meant that the world was waiting for the reign of man. . . . Above all that we see, above these ghost towns and these cities in ruins, a still more terrible presence is hovering over Europe. For ravaged and bleeding Europe is not more ravaged and bleeding than the face of the man it had hoped to bring forth."

Thus Malraux the "European" is the receiver in bankruptcy of the "new order" in Europe, which others before him evoked in the same desperate tone and which they would again like to foist on us with a few variations and a different name, "Western civilization." This "Western civilization" (in the Anglo-Saxon version) would drive us into the same bankruptcy as its European predecessor (in the German version). Malraux knows it, for he concludes: "Whatever humanism we seek, it is doubtful whether it will save us from war."

Who is bankrupt in all this? And what man is about to die? The bankruptcy is that of a decaying system whose reprieved corpse is still poisoning the "European world" (German version) or the "Western world" (Anglo-Saxon version). The man about to enter his death throes is the representative of a dying class: when this man, bound to a class, has that "conscious will" which Malraux glorifies, he can only grow conscious of these contradictions, these dead ends, this death. And he becomes a prophet of disgust and despair, with their evasions and opiates, a prophet of eroticism, opium, sexual perversion, terrorism, etc. . . . "All suffer," says the opium-smoking philosopher Gisors in *Man's Fate,* "and each one suffers because he thinks. . . . The consciousness of life can be nothing but anguish." There is no perspective or way out for this dying class, in which, in the words of a critic who admires Malraux, "each character grows conscious of himself in an experience that reveals to him the absurdity of the world and the abjectness of destiny."

To find the sources of these "idealisms" with their existentialist, "humanist," or surrealist variations, it is less important to go back to Heidegger or Kierkegaard than to see in them the literature and metaphysics of a world at a dead end.

Malraux's work gives us a striking portrait of the dead man, whose spokesman he is. His testimony is much more powerful than that of Sartre and complements that of François Mauriac in this literature of grave diggers.

POWERS OF THE DESERT

What, in Malraux, are the attributes of the dead man? First of all, he is solitary and he is eternal. Malraux gives us the most perfect formula for this in his *Days of Wrath*. Here is proof, if proof were needed, that it is not enough to choose a revolutionary theme to create a revolutionary work of art. Depicting the Communist Kassner, Malraux gives us the most *reactionary* allegory of man, in the deepest sense of the term. "The world of a work like this," he writes in his preface, "the world of tragedy, is the ancient world still—man, the crowd, the elements, woman, destiny. It reduces itself to two characters, the hero and his sense of life." There we have Narcissus comfortably facing his mirror.

In love as in war or revolution, Malraux's man knows only himself. In *Man's Fate* Ferral "never went to bed with anyone but himself, but he could do this only if he were not alone. . . . He would possess through this Chinese woman who was awaiting him the only thing he was eager for: himself. He needed the eyes of others to see himself, the senses of another to feed himself." And in all of Malraux's work "the others" serve no other purpose but that of giving the hero an opportunity to reveal himself. They fulfill their function perfectly

when they are tortured or in agony; Malraux needs the suffering of all in order to live violently. Almost all his characters
illustrate what might be called the "Nero complex": they enjoy
themselves only in slaughter.

Nowhere does the hero's power unfold in generosity: Katov
in *Man's Fate* gives his poison to his prison comrades in the
same spirit as that which drives Perken in *The Royal Way* to
the Mois and their torture. It is always self-glorification.
Garine confesses in *The Conquerors*: "I do not love men, I do
not even love the poor." And another character speaks in the
same vein: "Never have I felt as strongly as today the isolation
of which Garine spoke to me, the solitude in which we are,
the distance separating what is profound in us from the movements of this crowd, and even from its enthusiasm." Malraux
knows only visceral solidarity, the solidarity one feels in one's
own body. When Pol, in *Man's Hope*, sees the wounded pilot
get out of his plane, he "realized that everyone knew the
meaning of solidarity with his whole being." Elsewhere Malraux notes: "It was Magnin's first experience of the deep, almost
physical bond between the best Communists and their party."
The blows struck on the walls of Kassner's prison cell only
furnish an orchestration to his personal anguish. The presence
of others only serves as a catalyst for his self-revelation. The
heroes of Malraux's revolution continue the cycle which was
to have been initiated by *The Royal Way*: they are all "Powers
of the Desert."

In Kassner the Communist, it is not two classes, two forces
of history confronting one another, with all the originality and
marvelous newness that this historic drama can produce within
man in a given year and under given circumstances. No, it is
eternal man, exposed to obstacles as eternal as himself. These
obstacles may be the virgin forest, as in *The Royal Way*, or
fascism as in *Man's Hope*: they do not in the least change
"man's" relations with his "fate."

Action in Malraux is never rooted in real, historic oppres-
sion; nor does it ever attain a triumphant climax. Gisors "felt
the *basic suffering* trembling within him, not that which comes

from creatures or from things, but that which gushes forth from man himself and from which life attempts to tear us away." There lies the source, I would almost call it the abstract, mythological source of the initial suffering; and here, in *The Royal Way*, is the end point, which is not a solution but a kind of slaking: "Could he but break away from the drab and dusty life of those around him, and at last attain something beyond, something outside himself! . . ." Between the two, suspended in the void, reign man and his acts. Here is Perken in "action": "the infinite humiliation of a man caught in the snare of his appointed fate. Grappling with the prescience of his degradation, he felt a rush of sensual rage sweep over him, like an orgasm. . . . A grotesque notion flashed across his mind—of the punishments assigned to Pride. . . . He felt an insensate longing that such torments should exist, so that, in their extremity, a man might be enabled to spit in the face of torture, and defy it with full consciousness, with all his will, though it should make him shriek with agony. And such was his wild elation at the thought that he was risking more than death, so vividly did he see it as his revenge upon the universe, his warrant of release from man's estate, that he was conscious of an inward struggle, an effort to fight down an overpowering hallucination, a kind of ecstasy." There in résumé is the complete and "tragic" curve of André Malraux: from humiliation to frenzy.

In each of his works he begins all over again with the same indifference toward the ideals and social interests of his fighters, with the same skepticism as to the usefulness of their collective efforts.

MYTH OF THE ETERNAL MAN

But why, one may ask, after *The Royal Way* did he choose only revolutions as the backdrop for his personal dramas? The Napoleonic formula of his essay on Laclos gives us the answer: "Tragedy, in our times, is politics."

Man, eternal man, that is to say, the *myth* of man is here

torn out of its social and historic context. Politics is only a stage decoration; what *Man's Hope* tells us of the anarchist printer, Puig, expresses the essence of Malraux's thought: "He had always looked on the Spanish revolution as another Jacquerie. Since he saw no hope for the world, exemplary revolts were the utmost he could hope from anarchism. And so for him every political crisis resolved itself into a test of character and courage."

This theme is fundamental in all Malraux's work. Later in *Man's Hope* he again expresses it, this time in his own name: "The business of the revolution is to solve its own problems, not ours. Ours depend on ourselves alone. . . . No state, no social structure can create nobility of character, nor intellectual qualities; the most we can expect of it is favorable conditions."

Malraux has forsaken the revolutionary teachings of our eighteenth-century materialist philosophers, Helvetius and Diderot, who showed how our personal greatness depends on "social structures." At the same time, Malraux has broken with the great tradition of the French novel—the tradition of Balzac and Stendhal, of Maupassant and Zola, of Barbusse and Aragon. Man, in this tradition, cannot be understood apart from his environment, of which he is the highest and most subtle expression. The French classical novel was based on the physical man; Malraux's novels are based on the metaphysical man. That is why they lose all revolutionary content.

"Does there exist any premise on which the notion of man can be based?" the Altenburg intellectuals ask in Malraux's latest novel. (*Les Noyers d'Altenbourg—The Walnut Trees of Altenburg*.)

This metaphysical approach to man leads quite naturally to an aristocratic and reactionary conception of social life. Instead of humbly learning from the people, instead of watching man in the process of being born as did Louis Aragon when he wrote of the men of the Resistance as a "witness of the martyrs,"* Malraux muses on the tomb of "the dead man"

* One of the pen names of Louis Aragon during the French Resistance movement.

30

and continues the prejudices that have brought this man to decadence and doom. He continues to believe that it behooves a so-called "élite" of intellectuals detached from life, the philosophizing adventurers of his novels, "to create man" or "re-create reason."

Expect nothing of the people and their struggles; expect everything of the metaphysical onanism of this "intellectual élite," that is, of the tiny group of questioners and answerers he has set up in his books by multiplying portraits of himself. Such is the new edition of "the enlightened despotism" which Malraux offers as the last word of his political wisdom.

Man's Hope is dominated by this preoccupation: "Reason has to be rebuilt on a new basis. . . . The only hope that the New Spain has of keeping that for which you and Jaime and so many others are fighting is that somehow the thing which we've been trying our best to inculcate year after year may be preserved . . . the quality of man." After which this teacher of humanity pours himself out another glass of brandy (like Gisors smoking a new pipe of opium), and still fails to see in his alcoholic and metaphysical fog that a *new* man is being forged in the struggle.

Several pages further, in the midst of a people offering thousands of martyrs to win their right to live, another deca-dent esthete, Scali, asserts: "All the same, some men will have to be taught again the art of living. . . ." As if that were an intellectual's privilege, instead of his learning life from those who win life, create it, and who are ready to sacrifice it.

Four pages later this "man of quality" preens himself and defines the role of the "élite": "The only guarantee that an enlightened policy will be followed by a popular government isn't our theories but our presence, now and here. The moral standard of our government depends on our efforts and on our steadfastness."

We are reminded of Carlyle, of the hero and hero worship. That is where this line of thought in Malraux leads. In his November, 1946, lecture, Malraux declared: "The Church is

31

of no importance here, because in this domain the Saints are all-important; the army is of no importance because the heroes are all-important; and at bottom, students, it does not matter in the least for any one of you, whether you are Communist, anti-Communist, liberal, or no matter what, for the only real problem is to know how—above these structures—and in what form we can recreate man." As if the whole of intellect, with our reasons for living and the creation of man, were not being staked each day in our struggles for bread and freedom!

DESPAIR AS A REASON FOR BEING

This man, dead because he has divorced himself from the people, from their sorrows, their hopes, and their angers, this solitary and eternal man is a desperate man.

Malraux's world, the only one that exists for one who refuses to fight the existing order head-on, is that of despair. Malraux himself defines it in his preface to Faulkner's *Sanctuary*: "A world of only the crushed."

Everything in his books assumes the somber hue of fate, sorrow, or death. In his prison, the Communist hero of *Days of Wrath*, Kassner, is not sustained by the certainty of any ideals or by the presence of any "brotherhood of man" in the struggle. What Malraux wrongly calls "brotherhood" is only the echo of other despairs. In this desperate solitude, "his courage had assumed the form of death"; "hope itself was a form of suffering"; "what was man's freedom but the knowledge and manipulation of his fate?" For the trapped man of Malraux as for the beaten man of Sartre, hope and despair, clarity and absurdity become equivalent and identical. So it is in *Man's Fate*: "Deep down, Gisors felt hope, as he felt anguish, hope of nothing, expectation."

Malraux, the motionless and solitary Malraux, who has not undergone any evolution in a quarter of a century of adventures, wars, and revolutions because he has traveled over the world wrapped in himself, has not changed his vision of the world from his early *Temptation of the West* to his recent

Wrestling with the Angel: "At the heart of European man, dominating the great movements of his life, there is a basic absurdity," asserted the Chinese Ling in Malraux's first published essays. And he analyzed this absurdity, breeder of despair: "Despite its accurate power, the European evening is wretched and empty, empty as a conqueror's soul." No better definition of the moral decay of imperialist capitalism could be found. And the man who does not see any forces of the future rising up against it must come to the conclusion: "There is no ideal to which we can sacrifice ourselves, for we know the lies in all of them, we who do not know what Truth is." This world is aimless. And the life of a man, who does not struggle to destroy it with the clear-sighted vision of another social order, is a desperate life, a life which, rebellious and embittered, merely waits for death.

This grimace of life creates all the tragedy in Malraux's works. What pleases him in an insurrection is not its positive surge toward life, not its enthusiasm, but the intensity of lyric disorder which it substitutes for the routine disorder of the old regime. The intensity of this temporary disorder allows the individual to furnish variants of himself, to experience his potential personalities.

Disorder is indispensable to Malraux the negator. He does not exist and does not fight save against something—not for something. "I think," says Kyo in *Man's Fate*, "that Communism will make dignity possible for those with whom I am fighting. . . ."

"What do you call dignity? . . .

"The opposite of humiliation."

Then what becomes of dignity in a social order that is no longer humiliating to the mass of men? What would become of Malraux's heroes if there was nothing left to destroy? To them the triumph of a revolution would be a disappointment and a defeat: man loses consciousness of himself as soon as the apocalyptic frenzy of the battle ceases. This is the last word in what Malraux entitles, ironically perhaps, *Man's Hope*: "Some day there would be peace. And he, Manuel, would become another man, someone he could not visualize as yet."

There is nothing else in man's fate but enslavements and their negation. And man, were he to get out of this desperate situation, would lose his reason for being and his dignity. "Permanent revolution," Trotsky called it, falsifying an expression by Marx. "*Permanent* despair," asserted Stalin.

For of what use can action be if it is without content? Freedom, if it is without content? Existence without content? Consciousness, if it has no other content save itself? In a famous chapter in *Man's Hope* Malraux counterposes "being" and "doing." But the fundamental question remains unanswered: being whom, and doing what?

In Malraux action does not get its value or significance from the reality it transforms in society or in man. "It seems to me," Ling the Chinese asserts, "that you attach too much importance to what is called by almost universal consent reality." Action has no other end but itself: it is the art for art's sake of a human existence. "The soul of Europe then seemed to me to be creation constantly renewed by the activity of a world fated to act." (*Temptation of the West.*)

Sacrifice has no justification outside itself: "He who sacrifices himself participates in the greatness of the cause to which he has sacrificed himself. But I see no other greatness in this cause except in that which it owes to sacrifice. It is without intelligence." (*Ibid.*)

WHEN THE DEAD BEGIN TO SING

What counts in action is only the intoxication it gives. "I can no longer conceive of man independently of his intensity." (*Ibid.*) It expresses nothing else but what Perken in *The Royal Way*, speaking of a sexual experience, calls "flaying the senses to satiety."

With this nihilist perspective, attributing a goal to action means debasing it for it means limiting it. ". . . He had come to treat the lack of finality inherent in all life as an incentive, rather, to activity." (*The Royal Way.*)

The glamor of this adventurous activity is freedom. Malraux's freedom is twin to Sartre's: it is found at the breaking point of the human and its laws. It is to action what the orgasm is to love. When Perken advances toward the Mois and their tortures, his heart, Malraux tells us, is "fretted with longing for the liberty that was escaping him." Liberty is attained in this delirium caused by the nearness of blood, torture, and death. Freedom, which in Sartre confronts nothingness, is the corridor to death in Malraux. It is true that freedom is not alone in that, since everything in Malraux's works flows into death. Being and one's consciousness of being have no savor except in the hunger for death. Perken, one of Malraux's many aliases, confides in the young Claude:

"To live defying death. . . . Then you want to die with an intense awareness of death, and yet without . . . flinching?

"I've been very near death. And you can't imagine the wild elation of those moments—it's the sudden glimpse of the absurdity of life that brings it—when one meets death face to face, naked—stark naked suddenly. . . .

"You've never thought seriously of killing yourself?

"When I think about my death it's with a view to living—not to dying."

Death is the measure and salt of life. It is the end point and apotheosis of action, which is only a delayed suicide. This profound defeatism runs through all of Malraux's writings and gives them their reactionary stamp. To a revolutionary, it is not death but creation that is the measure of life. In Malraux action is merely a Pascalian amusement or, better still, an intoxication. It means forgetting an intolerable consciousness. But what is intolerable in our consciousness is the presence of an intolerable society—and the revolutionary role of action is to change this world, not to escape from the consciousness we have of it.

Ch'en-Malraux (in *Man's Fate*) achieves the perfect act, a well-contrived death:

"I shall soon be killed.

"Isn't that what he wants above all? Gisors wondered. He aspires to no glory, to no happiness. Capable of winning, but not of living in his victory, what can he appeal to if not to death? No doubt he wants to give it the meaning that others give to life. To die on the highest possible plane."

And in *Man's Hope*:

"Here in the front line it's a very different story. After the first ten days you're an automaton, a sleep-walker. You see too many men die. There's too much of the machine in what's against you: tanks, artillery, planes. Fate takes charge, and you're only sure of one thing—that you haven't a dog's chance. You're like a man who's drunk a poison that kills after a certain number of hours, or like a chap who's taken the monastic vow. Your life is over.

"Then the whole world's changed. You get a new line on the truth, and it's all the others who are off their heads. . . .

"Yes, that's how it is, one pushes ahead into the barrage; nothing, not even one's own life, makes the least difference. Hundreds of shells are falling, hundreds of men going forward. You're just another case of suicide, yet at that moment you're sharing in all that's best in all of them. . . . You're sharing in . . . in something that's rather like the ecstasy of the crowd at Carnival. . . . I've a pal who calls that the moment when the dead begin to sing. Yes, for a month now, I've known dead men can sing. . . .

"And there's something else which even I, the first Marxist officer in the army, never dreamt of. There's a fraternity which is only to be found—beyond the grave."

ERSATZES FOR DEATH

The annoying thing about death is that it happens only once: to weave it into the fabric of life, one must find ersatzes for it. This "ecstasy toward the depths" which death produces can be created artificially by opium, alcohol, drugs, terrorism, or adventure. All these flights are escapes which, for a time, tear us away from the grip of fate. The all important thing in this kind of living is for each individual to find the proper drug. Malraux says of a character in *Man's Fate*: "He drinks, but he was made for opium: it's also possible to choose the wrong vice; many men never strike the one that might save them." That is the only way in which we free ourselves of "primal anguish." Kyo, in *Man's Fate*, says: "My father believes that the essence of man is anguish, the consciousness of his own fatality, from which all fears are born, even the fear of death . . . but that opium frees you from it. . . ."

Gisors embodies this wisdom: "There is always a need for intoxication: this country has opium, Islam has hashish, the West has woman. . . . Ch'en and murder, Clappique and his madness, Katov and the revolution, May and love, himself and opium."

This ethic of decadence rules over Malraux's world as it ruled over the *Satyricon* of Petronius. Voluptuousness has the smell of death. When Perken made love, "he too closed his eyes, thrown back upon himself as on a noxious drug, drunk with a wild desire violently to crush out of existence this stranger's face that urged him on to death."

Let us not linger over this company of monsters; let us consider only Malraux's favorites: the terrorists. He prefers them because the raw material they work in is death. If one can die but once, one can kill several times and thus enjoy the orgasm of death. Ch'en enters into a trance as he is about to commit **murder**:

"You want to make a kind of religion of terrorism?"—Ch'en's exaltation was growing. All words were hollow, absurd, too feeble to express what he wanted of them.

"Not a religion. The meaning of life. The . . . complete possession of oneself. Total. Absolute. To know. Not to be looking, looking, always, for ideas, for duties. In the last hour I have felt nothing of what used to weigh on me. Do you hear? Nothing."

37

This adventurous vision of men shapes Malraux's opinions concerning revolutionaries: according to him, the International Brigades in Spain were made up as follows: "The sort of volunteer we got at first was usually a bit of a lunatic or a bit of a hero. Sometimes both at once." Elsewhere in *Man's Hope*: "The war assimilated mercenaries and volunteers alike in a romantic venture."

And it is in this sense that Malraux makes revolution mysterious. Action is not interesting except when it is studied as if at arm's length. Man faces his activity as an artist his creation: he is external and superior to it. Ferral, in *Man's Fate*, "wanted to be distinct from his activity—a way of considering himself superior to it." And *Man's Hope* develops the same theme: "A man devotes to any line of action only a limited part of hmself; and the more that line of action sets up to be 'totalitarian,' the smaller is the part of him involved."

So this master craftsman is as reassuring as he is attractive to the decadent upper class; he knows how to produce apocalyptic thrills, but with respect to action he is well-bred enough to hold it comfortably at arm's length. Only thus can the "élite" continue to claim their monopoly of things of the "spirit."

This Don Juan of revolution brings back a reportage from hell. But when you look at it closely, this hell is not dangerous. It is not the hell of the "wretched of the earth"; it is the hell which the writer bears in himself, his spiritual anguish. That kind of a hell is quite acceptable and far from explosive. Noble lords and gentle ladies, be grateful to the handsome juggler who has performed such tricks, such elegant sleight-of-hand!

CAREER OF A SOLDIER OF FORTUNE

But of course you must persuade everyone around you that this spiritual revolution is a "real" revolution. To accomplish that, you have to have an authentic witness. So Malraux becomes the "revolutionary type"—even if history does not confirm it, legend will. And Arthur Koestler, in his *Yogi and the Commissar*, supplies Malraux with the revolutionary halo.

This new transformation is as subtle as the first one. How is one to fit into the dazzling legend of revolution the real history of this desperate soldier of fortune?

His career and wealth began right after World War I, with a journey to the Far East in which a passion for archaeology, a spirit of adventure, and financial speculations were inextricably combined. Purified and appropriately presented, that exploit resulted in *The Royal Way* and *Temptation of the West*. His search for Oriental bas-reliefs brought him close to the upheavals of the Chinese Revolution. From 1925-1927 he was with the Chinese Kuomintang: his personal part in the movement consisted of organizing, with the Committee of Twelve, the adventurist Canton Commune, which ended in the slaughter of masses of workers and democrats. Fortified by this experience, which furnished him with the theme for *The Conquerors* and *Man's Fate*, he returned to France just in time to enter into relations with Trotsky, thenceforth his spiritual father.

In August, 1936, he arrived in Spain as head of the *España* air squadron, with a duly signed contract by which he got a double salary paid out in dollars in Paris and in *pesetas* in Madrid. This mixture of love of risk and mercenary preoccupations resulted in disorder and a breakdown of discipline in the squadron, which nevertheless did contain some truly heroic fighters for freedom. In October of that year, Malraux, refusing to bow to military discipline, left the squadron and the country. He returned to Spain as a movie producer. This was the period of *Man's Hope*.

By 1939, Malraux's anti-communism, already shown in Spain, was violent. This anti-communism, closely bound up in him with contempt for the common people, led him in the French Resistance movement to work with the British Intelligence Service instead of the masses.

After liberation he became a cabinet minister under General Charles de Gaulle. He was still collaborating, not with the people, but with those who despised the people.*

His life attests to the decadence of a social system and a class. His work is a testimonial to our times; but it expresses everything that is at present dying and in decomposition, not that which is coming to birth and growing. Malraux's "conscious will" gives us the consciousness of a civilization that realizes it is dying. His is a desperate conscience. An uneasy conscience, Hegel called it. "I do not consider society evil, capable of being improved; I consider it absurd." (*Man's Fate.*) Albert Camus speaks in the same vein. Sartre is filled with nausea by this world. In François Mauriac it inspires daily laments and novels whose realism throws a pitiless light on the baseness of a class. All of these writers give a metaphysical twist to the contradictions of a social system. Each of them attributes to an eternal man the contradictions they find in themselves, which are those of a class and a social system. That is the basis of the mythology which Marx called "alienation." It is a profoundly reactionary attitude because by projecting into eternity these contradictions of a specific period, it turns away from destroying their historic roots. The revolutionary attitude is just the reverse: if I realize that my problems and contradictions are the problems and contradictions of a social system, I shall only look for the solution of these problems and contradictions in the transformation of that social system. That is why dialectical materialism is the only basis for revolutionary thinking: it sees consciousness and its dramas only as the consciousness of a reality that is not altogether contained in myself. The world is not in me: I am in the world.

That is the first link in the great chain: if the reply to my anguish demands a transformation of the world, that transformation requires the participation of the masses of mankind. Only a real revolution will put an end to the unhappy con-

* Today Malraux is a leading propagandist and right-hand man of General de Gaulle.—*Ed.*

sciousness by bringing about an objective solution of the contradictions that the consciousness reflects and transposes. Only then is revolution affirmation and creation, not negation and revolt; only then is it joy, not despair.

To Malraux, revolution is not the solution of a problem, it is the opportunity for lyrical gestures. At bottom there is an unleashing of elemental forces with blind devotion and bloody sacrifices. In this somber apocalyptic-like setting flashes the lightning of "great personalities—with the masses as their step-ladder," in the words of Blanqui.

Conjuring up this disorder from the nameless masses, Malraux, god of chaos, draws from it the anguish of the "élite," the escapism of the privileged, the metaphysical alibi of a class at bay. This is precious alchemy for the ruling classes; they are ready to applaud all these transmutations, all these sleight-of-hand tricks: those of Sartre, those of Koestler, and those of Malraux. The main thing is to make a spiritual phenomenon of the revolution, a biblical paradox—"Wrestling with the Angel." At this level it no longer threatens the security or privileges of the few. Moreover, this "revolutionary spirituality" supplies a solid foundation to anti-communism. It is awkward and sometimes difficult to attack the Communists' national policies or some concrete phase of their activity —so blessed be the Koestlers, Sartres, or Malrauxs who are each at hand to offer noble, metaphysical, spiritual reasons for despising and hating the Communists in order to justify the struggle against them.

THE MAN WITH THE KNIFE BETWEEN HIS TEETH—1948 VERSION

All of Koestler's *Darkness at Noon*, the French publication of which was promoted by Ernest Bevin, is contained in miniature in a few lines of *Man's Hope*. An anarchist leads the attack: "I say that Communists are turning priests. For you, being a revolutionary means just being cleverer than the next fellow. . . . You're soaked in the party, in discipline, in plotting and scheming. If a man doesn't belong, you don't give him a square deal; you've not a scrap of decency toward him."

This concoction, this caricature has in present-day anticommunist literature replaced the gruesome image of the "man with the knife between his teeth," so prevalent in anti-Bolshevik propaganda after 1917. Our esthetes and sophisticates must be pretty frightened indeed if they are satisfied with that!

The Communist and his party in Malraux's books—except when Malraux blows him up with his personal philosophy as in the case of Kassner in *Days of Wrath*—is a wonderfully simple character, easy to hate. This mythological puppet obeys a single iron law: discipline, obedience. As someone in *Man's Hope* says: "Formerly, our people were disciplined because they were Communists; now plenty of people become Communists because the party stands for discipline." One thing is conceded to these robots: "They have all the virtues of action and only those." If war is reduced to this simple operation, "riddling the living flesh with fragments of steel," these human tanks are suited for it. But that is all one can expect of them and of the impersonal fate that guides them: the Communist International.

That is what the psychology of the "pure" Communist amounts to in André Malraux's works. But at bottom is there anything else in Koestler's Gletkin or his Bolsheviks? In reality, one doesn't have to bother about psychology with the Communists: it's enough to present a puppet, to set up a scarecrow and to instill fear. When it is a question of fighting the Communists, the refined esthetes are no longer so choosy. What matters the method chosen? What of it if it is vulgar? The main thing is for the Communist to lose all semblance of humanity! Once he is dehumanized, we are freed of all human obligations toward him: he is outside humanity's law.

In Malraux's works a person becomes a Communist when

his spirit hardens and his heart dries up: "What made you become a Communist, Ramos?" "Growing old, I think. . . . In my anarchist days I was much fonder of mankind in general. Anarchism, for me, meant the 'Syndicate'—but above all, human relations, human contacts." (*Man's Hope*.)

Here, according to Malraux, is the active Communist's rule: "From the day you take a commission in the army of the proletariat, your soul is no longer your own." (*Ibid.*)

You no longer have a right to use your reason or intelligence: "As a Communist, Manuel did not question the rightness of his decision; he had done what he had done, so be it!" And to give a stamp of authenticity to this condensed caricature, Malraux brings his "pure" Communist before a kind of Catholic father-confessor of active revolutionaries, Colonel Ximénès: "Every step I've taken towards greater efficiency, towards becoming a better officer, has estranged me more and more from my fellow-men. Every day I'm getting a little less human. . . ." And Ximénès ends on a note of triumph: "You'd like to lead men and yet remain their comrade; well, in my opinion, no man's big enough for that. . . . All that estranges you from your fellow-men is bound to link you more closely with your Party. . . ." (*Man's Hope*.) This is the type of reasoning that encourages attacks against all political parties, a theme with which the pro-fascist Charles Maurras and his present followers have made us familiar. Garcia, in *Man's Hope*, protests: "Yes, it's high time for everyone to realize that the masses are one thing, and parties are another."

And when one has manufactured such a mechanical, soulless Communist Party, one can only hate it: "You know," says Negus the anarchist, "the Communists are good workers. I can work with them. But as to liking—no! I've done my damnedest, but I can't get to like 'em!" So the next step is to refuse to "work" with those unpleasant robots—and that was exactly what Malraux did when he airily refused to have anything to do with the Military Committee of the Spanish Communist Party in 1936, or when he would not allow members of the F.T.P. [*Francs-Tireurs et Partisans*] resistance movement to participate in parachute-jumps with the British in 1944. These caricatures have a meaning: they furnish justifications for the most rabid kind of anti-communism.

ANOTHER "EUROPEAN" WHO SEEKS TO "ERASE '89 FROM HISTORY"

What is much more serious is that when he assails the Communists, Malraux is really attacking the whole French tradition of reason and progress, the entire revolutionary nineteenth century born of the eighteenth-century philosophy of enlightenment and of the high hopes of 1789 and 1793. Is it not curious how it is always the same men who, seeking "to erase '89 from history," always attack the Communists! Malraux the European, the Westerner, having dangled before our eyes his mechanical Bolshevik, then blithely condemns communism for the spiritual hold it has gained. He turns on reason, on progress, on the nineteenth century. In his lecture of November 4, 1946, at the Sorbonne, which has become a kind of manifesto for the followers of the fascist-minded Charles Maurras, he asserted: "I believe that European values have nothing in common with those of the nineteenth century. . . . At the present time, what are the values of the West? We have seen enough to realize that they are certainly not rationalism or progress. . . . The strength of the West is the acceptance of the unknown."

Malraux is haunted by the shadow of Nietzsche as Sartre is by the shadow of Heidegger; they are two variants of what was generally called some months ago "existentialism," which was only a new and barbarous name for the latest version of this three-fold contempt for reason, reality, and man, characteristic of all decadent modes of thinking.

And when this contempt has destroyed, within man and around him, all hope of the future and every chance of progress, the way is open to religion.

Fifteen years ago, in a lecture called "European Youth,"

44

Malraux asserted: "Our civilization, since it has lost hope of finding the meaning of the spiritual world in the sciences, is devoid of any spiritual aims." From that time on the Church was on the look-out for him. Mauriac was not wrong when, more than ten years ago, he made this analysis in his *Journal*: "Man, according to Malraux, prisoner of his materialist jail, shut up in a mechanized world, without any avenue of escape to eternity, finds his greatness only in despair; and with despair he loses his whole reason for being."

The Catholic Church knows how much it can get from these alchemists of despair who make of revolution a spiritual phenomenon, of freedom the tearing down not the building up of something that exists, and of disorder an apocalypse in which the human being asserts himself; it is well aware of the value of these magicians who exorcise everything it combats: science and joy. The Church does not burn these individuals at the stake as it once burned reputed witches. It utilizes them and guides them: they may smooth the path for a future believer. They are adept in steering an enthusiastic middle-class youth away from political activity and in leading him into such a blind alley of despair that the only thing left for him to do is to "stretch out his arms to the Liberator." O excellent propagators of the faith!

An editorial in the Catholic newspaper, *La Croix*, on December 20, 1946, entitled "To Save Man," is devoted to Malraux. Listen to this outburst of jubilation:

"André Malraux's lecture . . . marks an important stage in contemporary thought . . . by sincerely posing the problem of man. . . . It has been clearly demonstrated that science has not served mankind. 'Bikini replies,' says Malraux. . . . The atom bomb proves to us the bankruptcy of science. Drunk with its discoveries, the nineteenth century substituted science, which it considered all-powerful, for metaphysics. . . . Malraux is right to mistrust optimism concerning progress. . . . We share his point of view concerning the agony of thought in the past century. . . ."

And the author replies to Malraux's "anguished question" in the only way a question thus posed can be answered: "It is a question of restoring God to the uprooted helpless man of our time."

And that is the old familiar rut to which Malraux leads us! No wonder the fascist intellectual, Drieu la Rochelle, greeted him as "the new man." In reality, Malraux has not divested himself of the old man, the dead man he bears within himself, and which traditional religion has handed down to him. Here is how Ling the Chinese psychoanalyzes the "European" in *Temptation of the West*: "I cannot imagine, without being disturbed, meditations in which love with all its intensity is concentrated on a tortured body. And Christianity seems to me to be the school from which have come all the sensations thanks to which the individual has acquired a consciousness of himself. . . . I do not forget that your religion has taught you to study the world by basing yourself on the inspired consciousness of its basic disorder."

A MEDIUM FOR THOSE IN AGONY

Malraux's success arises from the same causes as the return to religion of the present-day bourgeoisie: Voltairian in the period of its greatness and church-going in the period of its decline. Malraux is a medium for a dying class and a dying social system because he furnishes a psychological transposition and a metaphysical justification of their disorder and agony.

The teachings of Malraux and those of the Church have this in common: there is no human solution, here on this earth, to our problems. The Catholic Church, as well as the ruling classes in general, ask no more than this of their thinkers: not to draw conclusions.

Our philosophers of the Intelligence Service are hard at work. In all of them we find the same false antitheses: in Koestler, darkness at noon, the Yogi and the Commissar; in

46

Malraux, being and doing, morality and politics. Furthermore, all the antitheses of our philosophers are found on the path of thought to action. "Always there is a conflict between the man who acts and the conditions of his action," Malraux writes in *Man's Hope;* and elsewhere, "Action . . . always involves injustice." Already our hero is perplexed and paralyzed. In this uneasy equilibrium of a social system on the brink of collapse, in which every real movement compromises its entire economy based on injustices and special privileges, on enslavement and slaughter, is there any doctrine more reassuring to the possessing class than this doctrine which teaches that the effective human being is a soulless brute (Koestler's Commissar) and that purity demands the renunciation of action (Koestler's Yogi)? Malraux, in a key chapter of *Man's Hope,* had already written that whoever wants "to do" ceases "to be" and whoever wants "to be" ceases "to do": "The Communists, you see, *want to get things done.* Whereas you (the Christians) and the anarchists, for different reasons, want to *be* something. . . . That's the tragedy of a revolution like this one. Our respective ideals are so different: pacifism and the need to fight in self-defense; organization and Christian sentiment; efficiency and justice—nothing but contradictions."

Effective action, political action dehumanizes a man. "You know very well, Monsieur Scali, how hard it is to be a *man,* far harder than the politicians think." (*Man's Hope.*) And "to be a man" one must break with those who want "to get things done." That is what is grandiloquently called: "attacking politics in the name of morals." In this vast metaphysical game everything is foreseen, even renegacy and its justification: "When an intellectual who was a revolutionary once," says Scali, "attacks the revolution, it always comes to this: he is judging the political methods of that revolution by his own moral standards."

It is characteristic of the ideology of a decaying class not to be able to conceive of agreement between man and the universe. The contradictions of the system are opposed to the

47

conscious mastery of the forces of nature. The world appears hostile to a society paralyzed by its inner disorder.

In this society the masters of chaos fear above all lest the contradictions be sharpened and then overcome. Unable or unwilling to conceive of a logical action being built on the ruins of its disorder, they retain only the negative side of this action, since to them it is only destruction. Then the antitheses between means and ends multiply, and all the elegies on how action destroys the delicacies of "the inner life." Action becomes the badge of louts if not of savage brutes. Once again aristocracy and distinction consist of not drawing conclusions, of not acting, of swaying endlessly between "yes" and "no," between purity and efficiency, charity and justice, victory and pity, the Yogi and the Commissar, morals and politics. This oscillation gives one an illusion of the infinite since it keeps on going all the time. And that is what our elegant decadents, "the most human men," in Malraux's phrase, call profundity.

THE SONG OF THOSE WHO LOVE THE FUTURE

As against the masters of chaos, there are those who love the future. To them, greatness is not in the consciousness of disorder and despair, but in the indomitable will to overcome them. "To make exploitation more intolerable by becoming conscious of the exploitation," Marx said; but our consciousness of the baseness of our present status is but the first moment in our action that fights against it.

It is in the name of this greatness that we fight against the reactionary defeatism in Malraux. The first chapter of his *Psychology of Art* sounds like a death knell: "The hope of a new art opening upon an open world has ceased together with the hope of a new science that was going to conquer that world. The European spirit, its vitality threatened, is undergoing a transformation—as the Medieval spirit, plagued by endless wars, went through its Inferno in the fifteenth century with the great lost hope of the cathedrals. Dying or not, certainly menaced, Europe—weighed down with rebirths it still embraces—no longer thinks in words of freedom but in terms of fate."*

Between the masters of chaos who like to think of the world "in terms of fate" in order to perpetuate its disorder, and those who love the future and think of the common people "in words of freedom," Malraux's choice is made. Ours is also made, irrevocably: against this aristocratic philosophy of dilemmas, against the tragic enticements of the dead man and Malraux, his embalmer, we choose a more down-to-earth philosophy, a philosophy that draws conclusions, a joyful and fearless ally of the forces of life.

Let us talk plainly: we see very well where this so-called "spiritual revolution" preached by Malraux, leads. A real revolution—the revolution—will be made neither by the Altenburg intellectuals nor by the newspaper *Combat*. These "spiritual" revolutions are nothing but an alibi for sidestepping the revolution.

---

* Quoted in the magazine, *Labyrinthe*, No. 22, p. 2.

THE LIE IN ITS PURE STATE:
ARTHUR KOESTLER

Nowhere is the mechanism of this general attempt at mystification more obvious than in Arthur Koestler. In his *Darkness at Noon,* that detective story with a metaphysical plot, the setting is concrete, but the problem is abstract, that is, false.

Koestler's entire case rests on a postulate: the innocence of the accused man who is the hero of his novel. He pretends to give a version of one of the Moscow Trials and affirms at the outset the innocence of his hero. According to him, Rubashov only sinned by intention.

But to set the facts in their historic context, let us cite testimony that bears weight: that of Joseph E. Davies, United States Ambassador in Moscow in 1938. In his book, *Mission to Moscow,* Davies writes:

"All these trials, purges, and liquidations, which seemed so violent at the time and shocked the world, are now quite clearly a part of a vigorous and determined effort of the Stalin government to protect itself from not only revolution from within but from attack from without. . . . There were no Fifth Columnists in Russian in 1941—they had shot them. The purge had cleansed the country and rid it of treason." (p. 280)

Simply by referring to real history, the falseness of the abstract problem is exposed. Would it have been an assault on human dignity to have executed Pierre Laval at the time of his first betrayals, before allowing him to sign the Montoire pact with the blood and slavery of thousands of Frenchmen?

At the time of the trial of Marshal Tukhachevsky, we were

told: Is it likely that a marshal can betray his country? Well, history has given its answer!

I shall not waste time describing the human setting of the Soviet regime such as Koestler depicts it: with its pack of monsters peopling the Russian inferno, its stuttering or hunchbacked Communists like Loevy, its drunkards like Ivanov, its morons like Gletkin, with an incoherent and insane Stalin, and the Bolshevik woman symbolized by Arlova, in whose mouth the author places the swinish phrase: "Do whatever you please to me."

Koestler suggests that in recruiting members for the Communist Party, abnormal persons are favored. Nor does he shrink from tales of madmen when he coldly narrates the story of the thirty agronomists shot because they asserted that nitrates were superior to potash as fertilizers. Has anticommunism paralyzed the critical faculties to such an extent that these zoological forms of anti-Bolshevik hatred are accepted without the batting of an eye?

But even that is not the heart of the matter. To describe to us the pangs of conscience of his hero Rubashov, Koestler has wrenched this conscience out of its objective context. And since he is working with documents, he is led to distort knowingly the texts in order to make unintelligible the attitude of the innocent man who confesses. But we have looked into Koestler's source: it is the stenographic transcript of the court proceedings of January 23-30, 1937, *The Case of the Anti-Soviet Bloc of Rights and Trotskyites*, which was held in the presence of representatives of the world press.

Koestler has taken his text from Bukharin's last plea. Here is what Koestler writes. Rubashov declares:

"There is nothing for which one could die, if one died without having repented and unreconciled with the Party and the Movement. Therefore, on the threshold of my last hour, I bend my knees to the country, to the masses and to the whole people. . . . Woe unto the defeated, whom history treads into the dust." (p. 240)

And here is the context, namely, the real statement by Bukharin when he was permitted to deliver his final plea. This statement admirably explains the real drama and gives it its meaning:

". . . It was not the naked logic of the struggle that drove us, the counter-revolutionary conspirators. . . . This naked logic of the struggle was accompanied by a degeneration of ideas, a degeneration of psychology, a degeneration of ourselves, a degeneration of people. . . .

"Every one of us sitting here in the dock suffered from a peculiar duality of mind, an incomplete faith in his counter-revolutionary cause. . . . Hence a certain semi-paralysis of the will, a retardation of reflexes. And this was due not to the absence of consistent thought, but to the objective grandeur of socialist construction. The contradiction that arose between the acceleration of our degeneration and these retarded reflexes expressed the position of a counter-revolutionary, or a developing counter-revolutionary, under the conditions of developing socialist construction. A dual psychology arose. . . .

"Even I was sometimes carried away by the eulogies I wrote of socialist construction, although on the morrow I repudiated this by practical actions of a criminal character. There arose what in Hegel's philosophy is called a most unhappy mind. . . .

"The might of the proletarian state found its expression not only in the fact that it smashed the counter-revolutionary bands, but also in the fact that it disintegrated its enemies from within, that it disorganized the will of its enemies. Nowhere else is this the case, nor can it be in any capitalist country.

"It seems to me that when some of the West European and American intellectuals begin to entertain doubts and vacillations in connection with the trials taking place in the U.S.S.R., this is primarily due to the fact that these people do not understand the radical distinction, namely, that in our country the antagonist, the enemy, has at the same time a divided, a dual mind. . . .

"Repentance is often attributed to diverse and absolutely absurd things like Thibetan powders and the like. I must say of myself that in prison, where I was confined for over a year, I worked, studied, and retained my clarity of mind. This will serve to refute by facts all fables and absurd counter-revolutionary tales.

"Hypnotism is suggested. But I conducted my own defense in Court from the legal standpoint too, orientated myself on the spot, argued with the State Prosecutor. . . .

"This repentance is often attributed to the Dostoyevsky mind, to the specific properties of the Slav soul (*l'âme slave*, as it is called), and this can be said of types like Alyosha Karamazov, the heroes of *The Idiot* and other Dostoyevsky characters, who are prepared to stand up in a public square and cry: 'Beat me, Orthodox Christians, I am a villain!'

"But that is not the case here at all. *L'âme slave* and the psychology of Dostoyevsky characters are a thing of the remote past in our country, the pluperfect tense. Such types do not exist in our country, or exist perhaps only on the outskirts of small provincial towns, if they do even there. On the contrary, such a psychology is to be found in Western Europe.

"I shall now speak of myself, of the reasons for my repentance. Of course, it must be admitted that incriminating evidence plays a very important part. For three months I refused to say anything. Then I began to testify, Why? Because while in prison I made a revaluation of my entire past. For when you ask yourself: 'If you must die, what are you dying for?'—an absolutely black vacuity suddenly rises before you with startling vividness.

"There was nothing to die for, if one wanted to die unrepented. And, on the contrary, everything positive that glistens in the Soviet Union acquires new dimensions in a man's mind. This in the end disarmed me completely and led me to bend my knees before the party and the country. And when you ask yourself: 'Very well, suppose you do not die; suppose by some miracle you remain alive, again what for? Isolated from everybody, an enemy of the people, in an inhuman position, completely isolated from everything that constitutes the essence of life. . . .' And at once the same reply arises. And at such moments, Citizen Judges, everything personal, all the personal incrustation, all the rancor, pride, and a number of other things, fall away, disappear. And, in addition, when the reverberations of the broad international struggle reach your ear, all this in its entirety does its work, and the result is the complete internal moral victory of the U.S.S.R. over its kneeling opponents. . . .

"Everything is clear. World history is a world court of judgment: a number of groups of Trotskyite leaders went bankrupt and have been cast into the pit. That is true. . . .

"I am about to finish. I am perhaps speaking for the last time in my life.

"I am explaining how I came to realize the necessity of capitulating to the investigating authorities and to you, Citizen Judges. We came out against the joy of the new life with the most criminal methods of struggle. I refute the accusation of having plotted against the life of Vladimir Ilyitch, but my counter-revolutionary confederates, and I at their head, endeavored to murder Lenin's cause, which is being carried on with such tremendous success by Stalin. . . .

"The point, of course, is not this repentance, or my personal repentance in particular. The Court can pass its verdict without it. The confession of the accused is not essential. The confession of the accused is a medieval principle of jurisprudence. But here we also have the internal demolition of the forces of counter-revolution." (pp. 775-78)

We came out against the joy of the new life. That is the real tragedy of the uneasy conscience. Its anxiety and despair are but the consequences of this bad choice.

That is the secret of all anxieties and despairs: one can build all kinds of mythologies and novels on this profound contradiction between the living movement of history and the personal attitude of escape or denial that one adopts toward it. They are the metaphysics of a class or a social order at a dead-end.

A world is being born, and I have been shut out—I have shut myself out. Can there be any greater despair?

I have shut myself out by this conception of freedom which uproots man from his past and robs him of all effectiveness, of all scientific and technical power over the real world to continue his future.

I have shut myself out by this attitude of negation and denial toward life, by this despairing philosophy of "No!" which multiplies revolts and robs us of the virile and positive joy of adherence and creation.

I have shut myself out by a conception of life that isolates and disarms the individual by mystifications of dilemmas without solution.

Koestler has tried to straitjacket us in the false problem and the false dilemma of the Yogi and the Commissar, of a soul without strength and a strength without soul, of darkness at noon, in which the individual can only be—all or nothing.

If Koestler advises us to swing endlessly between ends and means, he seems to have deliberately solved the problem for himself. His articles blatantly reveal to us his ultimate aim: destruction of the Soviet Union, of communism, of democracy in general, and that of France in particular. His open contempt for our country fits in with the declarations of Field-Marshal Jan Smuts concerning France's irremediable decadence.

As for the means, he does not dream of calling them into question. When it is a question of destroying what he assails with such hatred, a crusade and an atomic war of annihilation are the chief means he envisages. The apostle of the dilemma has once and for all made his choice.

THE ROAD TO LIFE

This profound hypocrisy reveals to us the scope of an offensive in which Koestler is in the van. *"They came out against the joy of the new life."*

In the face of these anxieties, true or false, I would like to make this personal statement. Many thousands of my comrades could make the same statement.

I AM A COMMUNIST WITHOUT ANXIETY

First of all, because I have not chosen to be a Communist. I have not chosen to be one, because it does not depend on me to deny the reality of the inner contradictions of capitalism, with its crises and its class struggle which is the motive power of its development. Since the days in which the analysis in Marx's *Capital* taught me the dialectics of history, I have found myself facing a compelling truth. Nor was there at any moment a choice between Marxism and its negators. Like Luther before his judges, I can say: "Here I stand, I can do no other."

Does that mean that we obey a rigid dogma, which it is forbidden to call into question? Not at all. A mathematician is not prohibited from calling into question the very foundations of geometry. But that in no way prevents him from calmly making use of the Pythagorean proposition; for he has the complete sense of security of the man who has made a decisive acquisition, the validity of which is guaranteed each day in practice. He knows that no "calling into question" of his geometry will smash this instrument in his hands. On the contrary, it will integrate this truth in a vaster and more comprehensive whole.

When Lenin, in his *Imperialism*, deepened the analysis of the contradictions of capitalism in a new stage, he did not demolish Marx's analyses. Nor was he satisfied merely to repeat them. He used them as specific elements of a more general science. And this new advance of the science of history furnished new insights into a reality that is every day more complex.

That is why I do not ask myself every morning if I ought to continue to be a Marxist. For I am certain that the capitalist system cannot escape its own destruction because of its contradictions, and that the class struggle, the motive power of history, will permit the working class to bring about the destruction of this system and the construction of socialism.

Let me give a concrete example:

In December 1941, when the German *Wehrmacht* was only a few miles from Moscow, when the C.G.T.* trade union movement had ceased to exist in France, and Communist Party members were being imprisoned or tracked down, we were deported to Southern Algeria. An inspector of concentration camps tried to get us to sign loyalty pledges to Vichy, pointing out to us the futility of what he called our "stubbornness." *At no moment did we think that we could be conquered.* Why? It was not at all a question of heroism or of a mass hallucination or of an act of faith. But we knew, we were absolutely certain, that whatever the length and horrors of the struggle, fascism could not stabilize itself. For no temporary victory can rid imperialism of its inner contradictions.

Is it a question of fatalism? I can hear the enemy saying with a sneer: "You believe in a fatal destiny which has been revealed to you by the prophecies of Karl Marx. . . ."

It is not a question of fatalism, because we are certain that "men make their own history," and nothing will be accom-

* General Confederation of Labor.—*Ed.*

plished without their fight. But that is where the second certainty comes in.

In his *Existentialism is Humanism,* Jean-Paul Sartre writes: "Since men are free and they will freely decide tomorrow what man is to become, tomorrow, after my death, some men may decide to establish fascism. And the others may be cowardly or negligent enough to let them do it. At that moment, fascism will be human truth—and so much the worse for us!"

We were certain, as we are certain now, that that is not true. Why? Because the same materialist dialectics of history shows us that at the very moment when imperialism leads the most reactionary and most chauvinist elements in finance capital to desire the open terrorist dictatorship of fascism, it leads the bulk of the working class, despite lies and betrayals, to wage a pitiless struggle against imperialism. That was why our confidence was unshaken: we knew that no matter how long the struggle lasted and whatever the bloody sacrifices, the working class, rallying to its side all the progressive elements of the people, would fight through to victory.

Our certainty was not based on our confidence in ourselves or on the abstract triumph of justice or truth, or on reliance on an élite of individual heroes, but on our confidence in the people—in the first place, its class-conscious and unshakable working-class vanguard.

I may be asked: but what is the role and place of the individual in all this? I reply: In this fight, the individual is neither zero nor infinite.*

My action is a necessary link in the chain of necessary struggles. The birthpangs of history require the participation of each individual—the advent of a new world will radiate all the more human warmth if each individual has participated in it with all his humanity. That is why I do not underestimate the personal contribution of each individual. And, I repeat, it

* The French translation of Koestler's *Darkness at Noon* is *Zéro et l'Infini.—Ed.*

does not depend on me to give or not to give freely of this joyful adherence. "Here I stand, I can do no other." When once I have understood what the world some day can become as a result of our efforts, I go toward that goal with all my strength and all my joy, with passionate attachment. "Freedom," said Hegel, "is the affirmation of self." By refusing to heed this doubly compelling certainty, the science of history and faith in the working class, I deny myself and the world. I want this certainty passionately, and cannot help but want it when I have become conscious of it. To us, as to Spinoza, freedom is this necessity which has become conscious, this creative participation in the dialectics of necessity which ushers us into a new life of an unsuspected fullness.

And what would my desertion or my betrayal be? True, any individual's defection takes some strength away from the movement. The rhythm may be slowed down; the color of events may be blurred. But their general curve cannot be broken. If I weakened, if I deserted the working class and its political party, if for a moment I was cowardly enough to doubt, others, I am sure, would immediately get new strength from their anger and contempt at my desertion to take *my* place as well as their own in the struggle.

On the other hand, having deserted the forces of life, what could such a renegade bring to the forces of death? Truths once glimpsed by us stick to us; and in my renunciation I would only have the unhappy and dual conscience of a Radek or a Bukharin. If my joining the Communist Party has been the beginning of my freedom, my betrayal would be the beginning of my agony, that agony which is always the price paid for a bad choice.

Reader, I am only giving you here a testimonial of my life spent in my party and its struggles for the past fifteen years. Do not come out against the joy of the new life. Let the dead bury the dead!

CONCLUSION:
DEFENSE OF FRENCH CULTURE

I have criticized the writer Jean-Paul Sartre for depicting only degenerates and human wrecks in his novels. Why is it that he always takes as the sad heroes of his works only men on the road to degradation, souls in disintegration, blurred consciences? He replied to me: "I can't help it, the world is like that." Whereupon I answered: "It is possible that men are *like that* where you go to observe them or spend time with them: at the Café de Flore, in the night clubs of Montparnasse or Montmartre. Such places may be filled with these dead souls, these aimless existences, these debauchers who can only brood over their impotence and their frustrations, in a word, the models you prefer in your literature of agony."

But there is another France, the France which showed in the *maquis* and on the barricades that it wanted to live and win out; which now, in the worst moral and material conditions, despite all obstacles and all campaigns of slander and defeatism, is continuing the same struggle against the same enemies, with the same courage and the same joyous certainty—at the work bench with tools, in the laboratories with formulas, in the fields with plowshares.

And there is no question about it: this kind of men, this manner of life can supply the artist or writer with themes and dramatic episodes that are at least as gripping as the others.

In truth, the artist's choice has a class significance. It is not determined by literary or technical reasons. The writer believes in this or that aspect of the reality he expresses. He can believe in what is in the process of being corrupted and dying, or else what is coming to birth, in the process of developing and growing.

The invasion of decay into art has a precise meaning: the class which had made culture into a kind of noble privilege has entered into a decadence beyond repair. The artist who has chosen to be the clown of a class in decay can only speak to this class of itself; and he will never reproduce anything but a more or less sophisticated image of this decay. The brilliance of his technique fundamentally changes nothing. How, without inspiring hatred and dismay, can one present to a dying world the image of the man of the future, of the joyful and conquering class that marches toward the future while sweeping away the powers of the past?

At every period in our literature, it is easy to find examples to illustrate this law. In the late eighteenth century, dying feudalism spawned a vast amount of pornographic literature as well as the most extreme forms of literary "preciousness," that is, the search for refinements in form devoid of all human content and thinking. On the other side rose up the young bourgeoisie, with a hymn to progress, reason, and joy, with a "philosophy of enlightenment," with faith in man and the future opening up before it.

Every class has the literature it deserves. The big bourgeoisie in decay delights in the erotic obsessions of a Henry Miller or the intellectual fornications of a Jean-Paul Sartre. In the chaos engendered by its decadence, it chooses to consider as the last word in its philosophy the doctrine of a Camus that the real is absurd and that the absurd alone is real. Yet this attitude is just the opposite of the rationalism of a Hegel who, more than a century ago, cradled the powerful dreams of this class when it was young.

Rotting capitalism has an art of rottenness. It presents itself in various forms. First of all, in a world in disorder which it is incapable of restoring to order, a decadent class praises skepticism. That is the surest way of prolonging the disorder so favorable to its privileges. Alain (Edouard Chartier) taught us "not to believe in anything" and "to form our opinions by a massacre of ideas." André Gide preaches "the gratuitous act," the "unattachment" (*la disponibilité*) of the individual who joins nothing and commits himself to nothing. Action is the enemy. "I am afraid of compromising myself," writes Gide, "I mean limiting what I could do by what I do." In the period between world wars, he was the perfect poet of man's decomposition.

Skepticism is only the reverse side of despair. And the literature of despair or "anxiety," as our "élite" calls it, is also very popular among our decadents. When the *Théâtre de l'Atelier* played Jean Anouilh's *Antigone*, there was standing room only; and the same was true in the case of the *Vieux-Colombier's* production of *No Exit*. When one leaves a play like that, there is but one logical attitude: if the world is really "like that," and if, as the author insinuates, there is nothing that can be done to change it, the only thing left is to commit mass suicide by jumping into the Seine! But this class no longer has the courage to commit hara-kiri.

At bottom, what it is looking for is an escape; to be diverted from the wretched impasse into which it has led the world, it likes nothing better than those who speak to it of something else, especially those who say that there is something else, if not on earth at least elsewhere—in heaven, for example.

That is the secret of François Mauriac's success. In twenty novels he depicts, with an excellent talent for observation and evocation, the ignoble features of a caste: that of the big merchants of Bordeaux and the large landed-proprietors of Les Landes. He knows this world well and scrupulously sculptures its traits in the mire. To console himself for such sordid humanity, he always tells us that besides this "sin" there is grace. But not here, not among men—in heaven, in God. That is his consolation for so much ugliness.

By the side of this escape into mysticism there is the illusion of adventure—in a Malraux, for example. What is a Malraux hero? At bottom, one of the despairing characters of a novel by Sartre who tries to escape his despair by a series of adventures and strong emotions. Instead of taking dope, smoking opium, or cultivating sexual perversions to forget the disorder of the world, he makes the rounds of revolutions. Not because he believes in them, not because he hates disorder, not because of class solidarity or because he understands the movement of history, but in order to get self-revelation from the spectacle of suffering and the intoxication of battle. From Shanghai to Madrid, and from the *maquis* in the province of Lot to the battles on the Rhine, Malraux seeks only himself. The smell of corpses and the frenzy of hopeless and aimless battles send this solitary figure into a trance and give him sadistic self-enjoyment. In him, heroism is a form of escape.

We have given but a few examples, which are all varying symbols of the same decadence: skepticism, despair, escape, all attitudes of a dying world. The trait they have in common is panic in the face of the real and, at the same time, the profound desire not to change anything.

Opposing them are the elements of a rebirth: those who refuse to make peace with what is the most sordid in reality. This point of view is not that of narrow sectarianism or a closed mind. The totality of the world is open to these new forces. But here the writer does not make his peace with decay; he does not have to turn aside if the manner in which he depicts it inspires revolt, not complacency, in us. And this revolt has meaning and value only if it is the prelude to positive, constructive action. A new man is being born. He is a poor artist indeed who does not perceive at least the outlines of his face.

The unfortunate thing about our age of transition is that the present system of education, which is a class system, has made culture a class privilege. The workers, who are in the vanguard of our country's rebirth, are not the ones who possess the literary means of expressing the heroic experiences they are living. And conversely the writer, usually molded by the bourgeoisie, has been cut off from practical social activity, from the world of labor. The artist found it easier to join the worker in the armed struggle than in the battle of labor; and that is why it is easier for us to have a literature of military heroism than that of the heroism of labor.

The experience of workers and peasants appears seldom in works of art, and its greatness has not been translated. The same man does not live this experience and translate it. That is why we note this divorce and this paradox: on the one hand, a wealth of suffering and of efforts that are not translated with the power of creative art; on the other hand, artists who have more means of expression than things to say.

While waiting for the indispensable remolding of man, we can at least ask the artist to dip into these human treasures from which he has too long held aloof. And we can at least give the reader the elements by which to judge a good book.

A good book is a book that does not leave the reader intact; it is a challenge hurled at us to change something in ourselves and in the world. A good book is a book that reflects something more than ourselves or the art of the person who has written it: it is a force, a tool or weapon, to make the dreams of today become the reality of tomorrow. A good book is a book that poses, with specific compactness and intensity of expression, a real problem for a real man in a real world. A good book is a fighting book, which helps usher in the new man. A good book is a book which does not separate its beauty from that of the real world it expresses, because there is no new art without new men.

A good book is a book that teaches us how to live and how to die.